INTRODUCTION

The nine year period of the English Civil War can be divided int
first Civil War, from 1642 until the King's surrender at Kelham
in which Nottinghamshire saw most of its involvement. The sec
with Charles' trial and execution in 1649, was little more than a series of loosely
related incidents during the summer of 1648 - the Battle of Willoughby being the
most notable local event. The third Civil War, fought for and by Charles II, led to
his exile after Cromwell's rout of the Royalists at the Battle of Worcester in 1651.

Nottinghamshire was a predominantly Royalist county, with many of the landed
gentry taking the King's side. Nottingham,
however, remained under Parliamentarian
command throughout the hostilities.

As Royalists and
Parliamentarians fought
to gain control,
peaceful villages and
busy towns saw violent
clashes between the
opposing armies. Many
families throughout the
land were torn by
conflicting loyalties,
which led to brother
fighting brother and
father fighting son.

This booklet forms a
guide to events which took
place in Nottinghamshire
during these troubled
times with biographical
details of some local
figures whose exploits
brought them national
prominence.

King Charles I

**Nottinghamshire
County Council**
Culture and Community (Reprinted 2000 and 2004)

PRELUDE TO WAR

The causes and consequences of the English Civil War have been the subject of much argument and debate for over three centuries. Charles Stuart became King of England in 1625. Although small of stature (he was under 5' tall), this proud man recognised that power lay in wealth.

Members of Parliament, anxious to retain some control over the royal purse strings, drew up a 'Petition of Right' in 1628 which prevented the King from raising taxes without their consent. The King initially agreed to this but frustration and anger with these financial shackles led him to dismiss Parliament by force and rule the country virtually single handed for the next eleven years.

The King needed to raise revenue from wherever he could. He fined people who did not attend church, forced the wealthy to give him loans, and most controversial of all, levied 'Ship Money'. This began as a tax on coastal towns to pay for warships but the King extended it to inland towns and used the finance raised for his own purposes.

Charles I believed in the 'Divine Right of Kings' and that he had been chosen by God to rule the country. But he was not successful. Archbishop Laud once said *''the King neither is, nor knows how to be great''*. With Britain's wealth and religion under threat, the struggle for power between the King and Parliament brought the country to the brink of Civil War.

Charles finally lost patience, and on 3rd January 1642 sent armed soldiers to arrest five leading members of the House of Commons who were proving especially obstructive. The King dithered just long enough for his plans to become known and when the soldiers finally arrived, Pym, Hampden, Haselrigg, Holles and Strode had escaped. *''I see all my birds have flown''* was the disgusted Monarch's retort.

King Charles I

Such an undiplomatic show of force sorely provoked Parliament. They refused the King money to fight the Scots who were invading England, or to quell an Irish rebellion, until they achieved their own aims of controlling the army, reforming the Church and appointing the King's ministers. Led by John Pym, Parliament openly challenged the King's right to rule the country.

King Charles opted for confrontation. He issued his call to arms in Nottingham and the Civil War began, a conflict which would extend to every corner of the land, divide families and counties, cost the King his life and lead to the country becoming a Republic or Commonwealth for the only time in its history.

THE RAISING OF THE STANDARD AT NOTTINGHAM CASTLE

Since William the Conqueror's time, a castle has stood on the massive rock which overlooks Nottingham. The original wooden structure was replaced by a huge stone fortress built by King Henry II in the 12th Century. It became a favourite of most monarchs but by the 16th Century, much of it was in a very dilapidated state.

On August 12th 1642, King Charles I called for "*all subjects who can bear arms northwards of the Trent and southward twenty miles*" to come forward to serve his cause. This was to be the rallying cry to the men of the county to join the King in his endeavours to march on London and retake it from Parliament. A week later the King was in Nottingham, staying at Thurland Hall, the Earl of Clare's town house. The ceremonial raising of the Standard* took place at six, on the evening of 22nd August 1642 before an assembled gathering of more than a thousand horsemen, soldiers, lords and '*gentlemen of his Majesties traine*'. Watched by the King's sons and his nephews Prince Rupert and Prince Maurice, a proclamation was read out and the fifteen foot long pennant hoisted on its pole. With a forceful gale blowing, the flag was held in position with great difficulty as trumpets sounded and cheers rang. out. War had been officially declared on Parliament. That night the Standard was blown down, "*an ill omen*" according to Clarendon.

GIVE CÆSAR HIS DUE

---

* *A printed report of 1642 'The True and exact relation of the manner of his Majesties setting up of his Standard', describes the Standard as "much of the fashion of the City streamers used at the Lord Mayor's show". The red pennant with its two long tapering tails was probably a 'one-off' design. It bore the Kings Arms quartered, a hand pointing to a crown above it and the motto 'Give Ceasar his due'. It is likely that the design also included a painted image of King Charles, along with elements of the Irish Standard.*

On each of the following two days, the proclamation was read again in the King's presence, but with the Standard being flown from Richard's Tower in the castle. The King's attempts at recruitment proved unsuccessful among townsfolk reluctant to become involved. After three weeks, only three hundred men came to the recruiting centre at the Salutation Inn, to join the Royalist Ranks.

The Salutation Inn, Nottingham

Nottingham Castle was not to become a Royalist stronghold as might have been presumed. With 20,000 Parliamentarians under the Earl of Essex threateningly close by in Northampton, the King and his followers left for Shrewsbury where support was stronger.

The initial confrontation between the two forces came at Edgehill on October 23rd. Sir Edmund Verney, the King's Standard Bearer, echoed the sentiments of many when he told the King's adviser, Clarendon, *"for my part I do heartily wish the King would yield and consent to what they desire. I have served him near thirty years and I will not ... forsake him; and choose rather to lose my life (which I am sure I shall do) than to preserve and defend those things which are against my conscience to preserve and defend"*. Maybe Sir Edmund

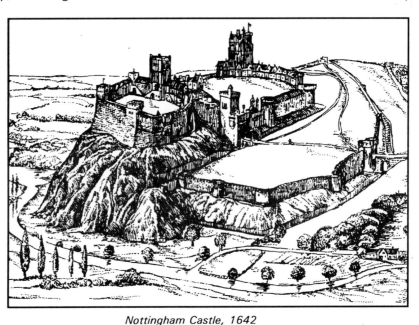

Nottingham Castle, 1642

chose not to avoid the fate he had predicted. Having refused to put on armour, he carried the Standard into the thick of the fighting at Edgehill. He was killed during the battle, but so tight was his hold on the Standard that his hand had to be hacked from his body before the flag could be triumphantly carried off by the enemy. Neither side could claim victory in this opening clash and a long drawn out period of civil hostility was about to become reality.

With the early stages of the Civil War being fought outside Nottinghamshire, the High Sheriff, Sir John Digby, strove to take the county for the King. By December 1642, Digby had occupied Newark, with Scotsman Sir John Henderson appointed by Royal assent as its Governor.

Prominent local Parliamentarian, John Hutchinson, was alarmed by this Royalist takeover of Newark. Fearing that Nottingham would go the same way, he rallied the town's inhabitants and enlisted 700 of them to defend it. Faced with such resistence, Digby held back. Support for Parliament grew in Nottingham and a Defence Committee was formed, which included Henry Ireton, who later married Oliver Cromwell's daughter. John Hutchinson became Governor of Nottingham Castle in June 1643. This was an unenviable job, given the ruinous state of the building and the quarrelsome nature of many of those around him.

Hutchinson raised a few eyebrows locally when, instead of trying to defend the town itself, he prepared the castle for siege conditions. He built cannon platforms and also allowed townsfolk who were willing to repair the castle to live within its protective walls. With Nottingham's entire stock of weapons and ammunition inside the castle, Hutchinson was as prepared as he could be for whatever was to follow.

When the war ended, Hutchinson oversaw the demolition of the castle, never wanting to see it used again in such a struggle. Nine years to the day after the Standard was raised, Cromwell rode through Nottingham to the Battle of Worcester. He declared himself "*heartily vexed*" after discovering that the castle had been dismantled.

Dismantling Nottingham Castle, 1651

Today's 'castle' is a Victorian reconstruction of the ducal palace erected by the Duke of Newcastle in the 1670s and severely damaged by fire in 1831 by Reform Act rioters.

NOTTINGHAM UNDER ATTACK

In September 1643, 600 Cavaliers from Newark led by Hutchinson's *'most uncivil enemie'* and cousin, Sir Richard Byron, stealthily entered Nottingham assisted by the treachery of the town mayor. Some of Hutchinson's soldiers had disobeyed his order to remain within the castle and were sleeping in the town. Many of them were surprised by the Royalists and taken prisoner. Hutchinson was left to try and defend the castle as best he could, although he had to contend with the constant bombardment of musket fire from the tower of St. Nicholas' Church. The Royalists also took Trent Bridge to try to blockade Nottingham from the south. They built a small fort with an eighty-man garrison commanded by Captain Rowland Hacker. For five days the Royalists plundered Nottingham until a relief force of 500 men from Derbyshire arrived compelling the Cavaliers to beat a hasty retreat back to Newark. The Trent Bridge fort continued to be held for nearly a month until it was abandoned when about to be stormed by the Derbyshire Parliamentarians.

Chastened by this experience, Colonel Hutchinson ordered the immediate demolition of St. Nicholas' Church to prevent it being used

St. Nicholas' Church, Nottingham

again as a base from which to attack the castle. The present day church built on the same site dates from 1682.

Colonel Hutchinson had to contend with a further raid by Newark Royalists in January 1644. 1,500 attackers led by Sir Charles Lucas ploughed through knee-deep snow to enter the town. With all the Nottingham Roundheads within the castle, the Royalists were easily able to occupy the town, but only for a few hours. Led by Colonel Thornhagh*, wave upon wave of Parliamentarian soldiers poured from the castle. They chased after the Cavaliers who attempted to set light to buildings by firing their pistols into the

---

* Colonel Francis Thornhagh (son of East Retford Member of Parliament Sir Francis Thornhagh) was, according to Cromwell, "a man as faithful and gallant in your service as any". He later fought at the Battle of Preston where he was mortally wounded. He was buried on the battlefield but his body was later brought to Sturton-le-Steeple for reburial in the church, where there is a memorial to him. Lucy Hutchinson depicts this close friend of her husband as a man of integrity and amiable disposition.

thatched roofs. The King's men were pursued along the cobbled streets surrounding the castle, towards the Market Place. As the retreating Cavaliers made their escape to the woods around the town, wounded men and horses *'left a greate track of blood, which froze as it fell upon the snow'*.

In February 1644, Newark Royalists and Nottingham Roundheads clashed again. Colonel Hutchinson had been forewarned of a plot to attack Trent Bridge by Captain Rowland Hacker's Royalists. In Colonel Hutchinson's words *"this being market day, Shelford and Wiverton had chosen 30 of their men who in disguises should come like women and market people, and with long knives, daggers, hatchets and such kind of weapons as they had under their cloaks"*. The whole plot was thwarted when waiting Roundheads turned on the Royalists and chased them back across Trent Bridge. Ten Cavaliers were forced off the bridge into the swirling waters below. Five were drowned and four taken prisoner, although their Captain swam to freedom. Lucy Hutchinson writes that her husband would have been happy if his soldiers had flung all their captives into the Trent!

Old Trent Bridge

Having captured the Royalists in disguise, Hutchinson regarded them as spies to be punished by execution. He threatened to torture them by tying burning matches to their fingers to wring from them details of the plot. The prisoners were later exchanged except one, Slater, a Parliamentarian who had defected to the Royalist side. He was court-martialled and executed.

Nottingham saw little trouble after 1644 and was held for Parliament throughout the remainder of the Civil War.

NEWARK

In 1642, Newark held a supremely important strategic position. Its bridge over the Trent was crossed by the Fosse Way and the Great North Road, both major links between the north and south. The bridge was controlled by a strong castle which,

Newark Castle

by the close of the year, had become a Royalist garrison and a focal point for their activities. The King's men occupied Newark throughout the first Civil War, thus keeping open the route between the King's headquarters at Oxford and his supporters in Yorkshire and Scotland. For these reasons Newark became known as '*the Key to the North*'.

Inevitably, Parliamentary forces made several attempts to capture the town. The first was in February 1643 and lasted only two days. Newark's Governor, Sir John Henderson with 2000 men, successfully fought off an attack led by Major General Thomas Ballard's vastly superior numbers. Royalist sources suggest that only one Cavalier was killed against 200 on the opposing side which also had 60 prisoners taken.

Throughout 1643, the Newark Royalists continually harassed the Roundheads in Nottinghamshire, and even in neighbouring Lincolnshire.

The Parliamentarians deemed an organised attack on the town to be essential, and made elaborate preparations to put it under siege. It was led by Sir John Meldrum, with an army of 2,000 horse and 5,000 foot, but it proved to be another Parliamentary failure. The King's nephew, Prince Rupert*, was sent from Chester to relieve the besieged town. On the moonlit night of March 21st 1644, Rupert's army assembled on Beacon Hill. With the panache for which their dashing leader was renowned, Rupert's men charged headlong into the valley below causing panic and mayhem within the Parliamentarian ranks. Newark's Governor, Sir Richard Byron, pitched part of his garrison into the fray and

Sir John Meldrum

within the day, Meldrum capitulated. This netted the Royalists a vast haul of enemy weapons including an enormous 12' long cannon from Hull, affectionately called '*Sweet Lips*'.

---

* Rupert (1619 - 1682) was the third son of Frederick, ruler of the German State of the Rhineland Palatinate, and his English wife Elizabeth, sister of King Charles I. The tall, dark prince, always ''clad in scarlet, richly laid in silver lace and mounted on a gallant Barbery horse'', was a hard soldier, famous for his cavalry charges which mowed down the opposition. He was greatly feared by his enemies. Prince Rupert was accompanied into battle by his pet poodle ''Boye'', later deliberately shot during the Battle of Marston Moor.

The third attempt to take Newark led to a siege which lasted nearly six months (from late November 1645 until early May 1646); with enormous hardships being endured within the town. When Newark's fourth Governor, Lord John Belasyse, took command, extensive and elaborate fortifications were already in place. Ramparts, palisades and ditches encircled the town, with two huge earthworks, the King's Sconce and Queen's Sconce, adding considerably to its defensive capabilities. Newark was thus thoroughly prepared when the siege eventually began.

The Royalist garrison of 4,000 men, was completely surrounded by some 16,000 Roundheads, but it stubbornly refused to yield. Conditions for the townsfolk deteriorated rapidly. Shortages of food led to horses being slaughtered for meat, corn and gunpowder mills closed down as Parliamentarians diverted river water to stop them functioning, and plague claimed scores of lives each day. The town even ran out of money and used its silver plate to mint its own diamond shaped coins.

Siege Coin

The siege eventually ended by direct order of the King when he surrendered to the Scots at Kelham. Newark had become a '*miserable, stinking, infested town*'. Although the townsfolk had already secretly sued for peace with Parliament in London, Lord Belasyse did not want to give in. The Mayor urged him to "*trust God and sally forth*" rather than yield. But the end had come. With tears of frustration in his eyes, the Governor signed the surrender terms. On May 8th, Belasyse and his dispirited soldiers marched out of the town. Plague ridden Newark was left under the occupation of Colonel John Hutchinson and was to play no more part in the Civil War.

An order was issued by Parliament for the earthworks to be removed and the castle dismantled. A large workforce was employed to carry this out. Within weeks the defences were demolished sufficiently for them to be of no further use, and the once-noble castle transformed from a mightly stronghold to a sad and battered ruin.

NEWARK'S GOVERNORS

During the Civil War Newark had four Governors:

Sir John Henderson was an experienced professional soldier who became Governor in December 1642. Both his tactical skills and the defensive earthworks he had constructed were soon put to the test. Major General Thomas Ballard attempted to take the town in February 1643, but the hard-drinking Scot was more than a match for him, inflicting a decisive defeat on the Roundhead invaders. Henderson was removed as Governor in October 1643 after heavy Royalist defeats in Lincolnshire had left Newark isolated and vulnerable.

Sir Richard Byron (1605-1679) was Henderson's replacement, having proved himself a competent commander during September 1643, when he led a surprise attack on Nottingham, holding the town (but not the castle) for five days. Eight members of the Byron family fought for King Charles from the outset, including Richard who was knighted by the King at Shrewsbury in 1642. Although described by Colonel Gervase Holles as *"in every way unequall to the charge he undertooke"* it was largely through Byron's efforts that the town was able to resist Meldrum's attacks during the second siege. He had ensured that the town's defences were strong, and the well supplied garrison capable of holding out until Prince Rupert's forces came to their rescue.

Sir Richard Byron

A Royalist defeat in October 1644 at Denton, near Belvoir Castle, may have undermined confidence in Byron's leadership. Also, Lucy Hutchinson hints at a disagreement between the King's Commissioners and the Governor. These were possible reasons why Byron was replaced by Prince Rupert's friend, Sir Richard Willys. Byron left for Chester where his elder brother, John, was Governor. Sir Richard succeeded to the title of Lord Byron in 1652. He then lived at Newstead Abbey until his death in 1679. He lies in the family vault at Hucknall Church, where there is a marble memorial to his memory.

Sir Richard Byron's Memorial

Sir Richard Willys (1614-1690) was the third of Newark's Governors and, like his predecessor was knighted at Shrewsbury in 1642. His appointment came in January 1645, and was almost certainly due to the influence of Prince Rupert. But Willys did not impress the King. His failure to co-operate with the King's Commissioners was noted with Royal displeasure. When his Majesty came to Newark in the October, Willys publicly offended him by waiting at the castle gate to receive him rather than riding out to meet him, as he did when Prince Rupert arrived in disgrace after surrendering Bristol. Following the quarrel with his nephew, Rupert, the King seized the opportunity to replace Willys with Lord Belasyse. Enraged by this, Willys challenged Belasyse to a duel which was only avoided by the intervention of his friends.

Willys was one of the founder members of the 'Sealed Knot', formed in 1653 to co-ordinate Royalist activities during Cromwell's rule. After the Restoration in 1660, Sir Richard spent his remaining thirty years in the privacy of his country house at Fen Ditton near Cambridge.

Sir John Henderson   Lord Belasyse   Sir Richard Willys

Lord John Belasyse (1614-1689). When John Belasyse became Governor, the town was facing its darkest hour. Without delay, he directed a surge of furious activity to strengthen further the town's massive earthworks, although the formidable King's and Queen's Sconces were almost certainly complete by then. In November, Colonel General Poyntz took for Parliament the Royalist garrisons at Shelford Manor and Wiverton Hall. Joining forces with the Earl of Leven he put Newark under siege, surrounding it with sixteen thousand men. Belasyse was not completely on the defensive, however, and with Royalist sallies, forced the Parliamentarians to construct defensive earthworks of their own to protect their positions. The Royalists held firm throughout, although Belasyse no doubt viewed with dismay the desperate privations suffered by the besieged townsfolk.

Late in April 1646 Belasyse received a Royal Command. The King secretly informed the Governor that he was leaving Oxford in disguise and travelling to Newark to surrender to the Scots, camped near Kelham. Meanwhile, Belasyse was to draw up the best terms of surrender that he could. According to Samuel Pepys, the King's secret was *'wrapped up in lead'*, swallowed, and conveyed by the bizarre methods of *'the messenger's belly'*!

The King gave himself up on 5th May 1646. With a sad heart Belasyse left Newark three days later. Ironically, Belasyse was to join up again with Sir Richard Willys in 1653 as one of the six original members of the Sealed Knot. He died in 1689, his memorial in the Church of St. Giles-in-the-Fields in London tells how as *'Governor of Newark he valiantly defended that garrison against the English and Scottish armies till his Majesty came in person to the Scottish quarters and commanded the surrender of it'*.

THE GOVERNOR'S HOUSE

The timber framed, late medieval building which, according to tradition, was the headquarters of Newark's Governors between 1643 and 1646, stands on the corner of Stodman Street and the Market Square.

In October 1645, a violent quarrel took place in the house between King Charles I and his nephew Prince Rupert. Eighteen months earlier, Rupert was the Royalist hero who had relieved Newark during the town's second siege. Now, after surrendering at Bristol*, he found himself dismissed and disgraced by his Royal uncle who was suspicious that he had been deliberately betrayed. King and nephew eventually reconciled their differences to a degree but, a few days later, arguments flared up again with a vengeance. The King had decided to replace Rupert's friend, Sir Richard Willys with Lord John Belasyse as Newark's Governor. Rupert felt that this had

Governor's House

Rupert and Charles at the Governor's House

been done out of spite, and further angry words were exchanged with the King, who ordered the Prince from his presence. The following day Rupert, Sir Richard Willys, and his officers, left Newark for good, watched from an upstairs window of the Governor's house by the disconsolate King, *'weeping to see them as they went'*.

---

* During August 1645, Bristol was under siege, blockaded by both land and sea, but Prince Rupert assured the King that he could hold the town for several months. King Charles regarded Bristol as a valuable asset, and was furious when he heard that his nephew had surrendered it. Rupert, for his part, had little choice, given the alternative of certain defeat and massive slaughter. The King threatened to send Rupert 'somewhere beyond the seas' but, determined to have his say, Rupert, his brother Maurice and some one hundred and twenty officers headed for Newark, contrary to the King's wishes.

NEWARK CASTLE

Newark Castle, 1676

The 12th Century castle was built by Alexander, Bishop of Lincoln. Described as '*a magnificent castle of very ornate construction*' it was a rectangular stronghold with either a square or hexagonal tower at each corner, and an imposing gatehouse on the northern side.

For over three years of Civil War, the castle remained Nottinghamshire's strongest and most important Royalist garrison, frequently bombarded by Roundhead cannonballs, the scars from which are still evident today on the outer walls.

QUEEN HENRIETTA MARIA'S HOUSE

With the threat of Civil War looming large, Queen Henrietta Maria, King Charles I's devoted French wife, set sail for Holland in February 1642. She took caskets jewels with her to sell to buy arms and ammunition. Whilst there, she enlisted a number of professional soldiers who returned with her to England to fight for the King. Her return was fraught with danger when her ship was bombarded with gunfire from four Parliamentarian 'Men o' War' as she stepped ashore at Bridlington.

After a lengthy stay in York, where she was treated in lavish style typical of her wealthy host William Cavendish, Henrietta Maria arrived in Newark on 16th June 1643. It is thought that she stayed at the residence of Lady Leeke, wife of Royalist Colonel Charles Leeke who was later killed leading an attack at Balderton. The half timbered house on Kirkgate, Newark, can still be seen today.

Henrietta Maria's House, Newark

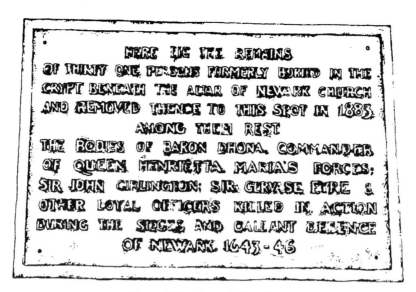

Memorial to Newark Cavaliers

Before leaving Newark for Oxford, some of the Queen's army took part in a raid on Nottingham. A German nobleman, Baron Dhona, led the force but was killed by cannon fire from Nottingham Castle. He was buried in Newark Church, but during the 19th Century his remains, along with other Royalist officers were reburied in the churchyard. A plaque* marks their final resting place.

The Queen remained in Newark for nearly a month before travelling to Oxford. There she was reunited with her husband on 14th July. With events so far going much the King's way, this was to be her triumphant hour. Her remaining twenty-five years were, however, destined to be full of unhappiness. She was soon to be in exile. Pursued relentlessly by the Earl of Essex, the Queen was forced to flee the country. Her escape via Falmouth was in the stinking hold of a Dutch ship. She was never to see King Charles again.

HERCULES CLAY'S HOUSE

Newark was under siege in March 1644, being continually bombarded by cannon fire from Sir John Meldrum's Roundhead army, who were completely surrounding the town.

Opposite the Governor's house stood the home of the Mayor, Alderman Hercules Clay. On three occasions Clay dreamt that his house would be destroyed. Fearing that his premonitions were about to become reality, Clay took his family away to another part of the town. Soon afterwards an explosive grenade, aimed at the Governor's House from the direction of Beacon Hill, smashed into Clay's residence instead.

In gratitude for the 'divine deliverance' of his family, Clay left money, not only for the poor, but also for an annual sermon to be preached each year in the church on 'Deliverance Day', March 11th, a tradition that is still kept. Clay died early the following year and is buried beneath the marble memorial to him in the south chancel aisle of the great church of St. Mary Magdalene, Newark.

---

* The plaque mentions Sir Gervase Eyre, ''esteemed as one of the best horsemen in the King's army'', who is thought to be buried in the parish church at Rampton. A small brass plate on the chancel wall there indicates that 'in this vault lie the remains of Sir Gervase Eyre, Esq., Knight who was killed in defending Newark Castle for King Charles I'. Newark Parish Church Register also records his burial on 5th May 1644.

ST. MARY MAGDALENE'S CHURCH

The two hundred and thirty foot spire of St. Mary Magdalene's Church would have been a familiar landmark to both Cavalier and Roundhead throughout the Civil War. It was badly damaged during the sieges but extensively repaired soon afterwards. A small plaque on a column tells how the font was destroyed '*by ye rebels*' on May 9th 1646, but restored in 1660 with a donation from a certain Nicholas Ridley. From the churchyard on the north side of the building can clearly be seen the large hole in the church spire, thought to be the result of a direct hit by a cannonball during Meldrum's siege.

Church of St. Mary Magdalene, 1676

SIEGE MONEY

Just before the third siege of Newark began, a mint was set up in the castle to meet the urgent need for money. Royalist gentry from both Newark and beyond, freely donated their plates, drinking cups and other silverware. These were beaten flat and roughly cut into diamond shaped pieces. The obverse side bore a crown with the letters CR and the value of the coin in Roman numerals beneath - 6, 9, 12 or 30 pence. On the reverse of each coin is the abbreviation 'OBS' (from the Latin 'obsessum' meaning 'besieged'), Newark and the year 1645 or 1646.

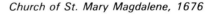

Siege Money

It was not uncommon for families to bury valuables as a means of protecting them until danger passed. Sometimes the items remained buried for centuries. One such 'hoard', over 400 coins, along with a silver thimble and sealing wax case, were all buried in a brown glazed jug during the Civil War. They were discovered at Crankley Point near South Muskham in 1957. More recently in 1988, a second hoard was discovered near Caunton. One thousand five hundred and seventy one silver coins dated between 1556 and 1644 were found, with a face value of £12 14s 9d. How and why they came to be there can only be a matter of speculation.

Coin Hoard, Newark Museum

Both coin hoards, along with examples of siege money, can be seen in Newark Museum on Appleton Gate.

THE SCONCES

When the massive Parliamentarian assault on Newark came in November 1645, the town was surrounded by a high parapet and ditch, with small forts along its length. Two 'sconces' (the Dutch word for a 'fort') constructed to the north and south of the town further strengthened the defensive fortifications. Townspeople were compulsorily recruited to build these structures, with fines if they failed to appear for work.

King's Sconce (adapted from Clampe's Siege Plan)

The '*King's Sconce*' was built on the 'Spittal', the site of a medieval hospital which stood between Northgate and the river, half a mile north-east of the castle. Described as '*a very noble and strong work*', the sconce had a house built in the centre of it, as Richard Clampe's siege plan clearly shows. The earthwork survived until its destruction at the end of the 19th Century.

The '*Queen's Sconce*', similar in shape and size, has survived and can be seen in Devon Park. The sconce covers about three acres and is encircled by a ditch 70' wide and 15' deep. At each corner are square bastions or cannon platforms which give the structure its distinctive shape. From these four bastions the sconce and surrounding land could be defended from all directions.

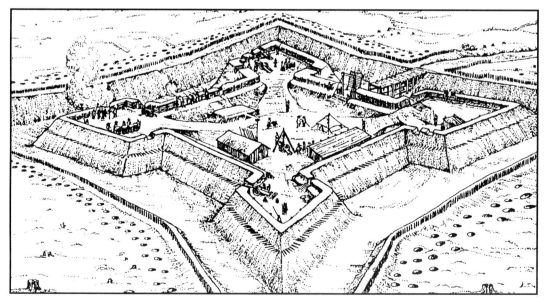

Queen's Sconce, Newark, 1645

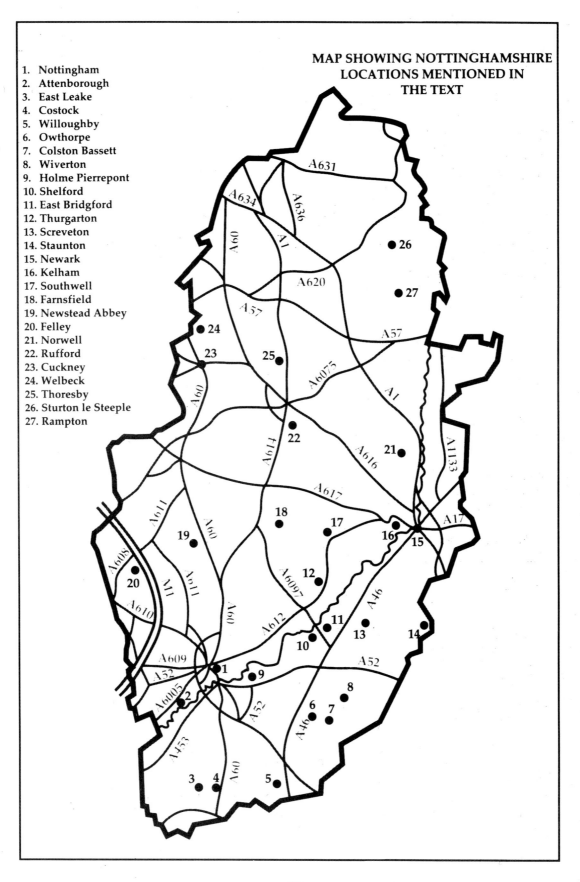

1. Nottingham
2. Attenborough
3. East Leake
4. Costock
5. Willoughby
6. Owthorpe
7. Colston Bassett
8. Wiverton
9. Holme Pierrepont
10. Shelford
11. East Bridgford
12. Thurgarton
13. Screveton
14. Staunton
15. Newark
16. Kelham
17. Southwell
18. Farnsfield
19. Newstead Abbey
20. Felley
21. Norwell
22. Rufford
23. Cuckney
24. Welbeck
25. Thoresby
26. Sturton le Steeple
27. Rampton

MAP SHOWING NOTTINGHAMSHIRE
LOCATIONS MENTIONED IN
THE TEXT

THE HUTCHINSONS OF OWTHORPE

The tiny hamlet of Owthorpe was home to the Hutchinson family during the 17th Century. We are given a clear insight into the life of John Hutchinson, the Parliamentarian Governor of Nottingham Castle, as seen through the eyes of his devoted wife, Lucy, who penned her famous memoirs after his death.

John Hutchinson was born in 1615 in Nottingham. His father, Sir Thomas Hutchinson, was a member of the House of Commons, his sympathies being with Parliament. His mother was the sister of Sir John Byron of Newstead, whose sons became closely involved with the events of the Civil War on the Royalist side.

After a university education studying law at Cambridge, John Hutchinson lived the life of a dilettante in London until he met Lucy, daughter of Sir Allen Apsley, Lieutenant of the Tower of London. Lucy was born at the Tower in 1620. She was a studious, intelligent child *"by the time I was four ..... I read English perfectly"*. After three years of marriage they moved from London to the Hutchinson family home at Owthorpe. They were *'happy in their own house till the Kingdom began to blaze out with the long conceived claim of Civil War'*.

Colonel John Hutchinson

Lucy Hutchinson

John and Lucy Hutchinson, both Puritans, were highly critical of the way King Charles was ruling the country. An incident in August 1642 drew Hutchinson into the centre of the growing conflict in Nottingham. Lord Newark (the Lord Lieutenant of Nottinghamshire), Sir John Digby (the High Sheriff) and some of the King's supporters, came to take the county store of ammunition and gunpowder. They were in the process of removing the arms when Hutchinson ordered them to stop. At first they ignored his demands but when he returned shortly afterwards with an angry group of townspeople *'prepared to lose their blood'*, Lord Newark eventually backed down, warning Hutchinson that he would thereafter be *'a marked man'*. According to Lucy, her husband carried *"an awe in his presence that his enemies could not withstand"*.

Hutchinson was, in some ways, an untypical Roundhead - reserved by nature, polite in manner, fashionable in dress and with his thick hair *"curling into loose greate rings at the ends"*. He had friends and relatives in both armies. His younger brother George, extrovert and popular, fought beside him throughout the war and married Lucy's younger sister, Barbara. His mother's family, the Byron's, were all *'passionately the King's'* - so too was Lucy's eldest brother, another Sir Allen Apsley. By Lucy's account, Hutchinson treated his enemies well, even insisting on entertaining some of the prisoners to supper. Lucy too saw much of the action, busily acting as nurse at Nottingham castle.

Hutchinson defended Nottingham with great vigour and authority throughout the perilous years of the first Civil War. Drunkenness, swearing and trouble making were punished by imprisonment. He was elected as Member of Parliament for Nottingham in 1646 spending much time in London where he was joined later by Lucy and their children.

In November 1648, with Cromwell in command in the north and Ireton's forces occupying London, Colonel Pride was sent to Westminster to throw out all Presbyterian Members of Parliament.

This left only fifty hardline Parliamentarians, the 'Rump' who nominated 135 commissioners or judges to try the King. Less than half of these attended the trial which found the King guilty. With Cromwell shouting down the waverers, fifty-nine of the commissioners signed a warrant condemning the King to death. The thirteenth to sign was John Hutchinson. Lucy tells how he prayed for guidance *"and finding ... a confirmation in his conscience that it was his duty to act as he did, he ... proceeded to signe the sentence against the King"*.

Cromwell dissolved the Rump Parliament in 1652 with his immortal words *"In the name of God, go"*, and the Hutchinsons returned to Owthorpe. There they rebuilt the hall, laid out extensive gardens with trees, canals and fishponds, and built the small church to be seen today, in place of a larger one standing on the same site.

Owthorpe Hall

The 1650s was a decade of happiness for the family. The Colonel played his viol, went hawking and educated his children, relishing the *"freedome in the country life ..... where innocence and safe delights abound"*. But these safe delights were soon over. The Restoration of Charles II in 1660 was in reality a death sentence for the regicides, Hutchinson included. Lucy, convinced that her husband would not defend himself adequately, wrote a letter to the speaker of the House of Commons pleading his case. Adopting his handwriting style and using his signature, Lucy's letter, along with Hutchinson's declared support for King Charles II, enabled the Colonel to avoid death.

Owthorpe Church

The reprieve was short lived. On the 11th October 1663, *"as bitter a stormie, pitchie, dark, blacke raynie night, as anie that came that yeare"* soldiers arrived and took the Colonel away to Newark where he was thrown into *'a most vile roome'* at the Talbot Inn (later called the Clinton Arms). Falsely accused by the Duke of Buckingham of implication in the 'Northern Plot' against King Charles II, Hutchinson was taken to the Tower of London. After six months of harsh treatment there he was transferred to Sandown Castle in Kent. Lucy rented rooms nearby and visited her husband regularly, but whilst she was away in Owthorpe fetching her children, the Colonel caught a fever* among the rat infested dungeons of the old castle and died on September 11th 1664. His body was brought back to Owthorpe for burial beneath the north wall of the church. The monument in the church bears an inscription thought to have been written by Lucy Hutchinson, but the year of his death is incorrectly given as 1663.

Hutchinson Memorial, Owthorpe Church

After the Colonel's death, Lucy began her famous 'Memoirs' written specifically for her children, to vindicate her husband's memory. These writings have recorded many incidents of the conflict in Nottinghamshire for posterity, and give us a revealing account of a county plunged into the confusions of civil strife.

Lucy outlived her husband by at least eleven years, but her widowhood was overshadowed by some loss of respect within her family. Her Royalist half-brother, Charles, bought Owthorpe Hall but showed little sympathy towards the regicide's family. The Hall passed out of the family during the 18th Century and was demolished in the early 1800s after being *'in a deserted state'* for many years.

---

* Lucy suggests the possibility that he may even have been poisoned.

243

brought severall gentlemen prisoners into the Garrison
of Nottingham which were taken in divers encounters
there when he marcht out Palmer the Priest not
daring to venture himselfe in the field layd downe
his Commission when he saw that there was now no more
conivance to be found at disobeying comands.

By reason of the Rout at Naseby and the surrender
of Carlisle to the Scotts and severall other Garrisons the
broken forces of the Cavalliers had all repayrd to Newark
and that was now become the strongest and best fortified
Garrison the King had and Poynts was Ordered to
Quarter his horse about it till the Scotts should come
to besiege it on the other side (at that time allso the
King himselfe was there) the Governor having informd
Poynts how preiudiciall it would be to his designe to
suffer those little Garrisons in the Vale at Shelford &
Wiverton to remaine it was agreed that all the forces
should take them in in their way but the Governor
having obteind permission of Poynts through a respect
he had to the famely sent to Coll. Phillip Stanhope
Governor of Shelford a letter to perswade him to surrender the place he could not hold and to offer him
to obtaine honorable termes for him if he would hearken
to propositions Stanhope returnd a very scornfull
huffing replie in which one of his expressions was
that he should lay Nottingham Castle as flatt as a
pancake & such other bravadoes which had bine
well enough if he had done anything to make them
good hereupon the whole force marcht against the place
and the severall posts were assignd to the severall
Colonells and the Governor according to his owne desire
had that which seemd most difficult assignd him
and his quarters that night appoynted in Shelford
Towne but when he came thither a few of Shelford
souldiers were gotten into the steeple of the Church
and from thence so playd upon the Governors men
that they could not quietly take up their quarters

The Governor Coll. Hutchinson

Extract from the manuscript of Lucy Hutchinson's "Memoirs"
(by courtesy of City of Nottingham Museums: Brewhouse Yard Museum)

HENRY IRETON OF ATTENBOROUGH

In the shadow of the tall spire of Attenborough Parish Church stands Ireton House, which incorporates the 17th Century building once owned by the Ireton family. Henry Ireton was born here in 1611, the son of a Derbyshire country gentleman. He graduated from Trinity College, Oxford in 1629, and studied law but chose not to pursue that career.

Ireton House, Attenborough

Ireton's political sympathies lay firmly with Parliament, and when a Defence Committee was appointed in Nottingham in 1642, he became a member of it. He rose rapidly through the ranks of the Parliamentarian army to become of of its most senior military and political officers. He was an able soldier, who fought with distinction firstly at Edgehill and then at Gainsborough under Oliver Cromwell. During the Battle of Naseby, Ireton was taken prisoner after *'being thrust through the thigh with a pike and wounded in the face with a halberd'*. He soon recovered, escaped and took part in the siege of Bristol in September 1645.

In 1646 Ireton married Oliver Cromwell's twenty-one year old daughter, Bridget, at Hollin House, near Oxford. The close friendship between Ireton and Cromwell assumed considerable political importance over the next four years.

Ireton, *'a melancholic, reserved dark nature, who communicated his thoughts to very few'*, revealed his *'unmerciful and bloody'* character after the siege of Colchester in 1648. He demanded the deaths of Sir Charles Lucas and Sir George Lisle, as part of the surrender terms, and indeed led them out to their place of execution.

Ireton is best remembered for his part in the trial of King Charles I. After the King had fled to the Isle of Wight, Ireton became convinced that it was not possible to come to terms with him, and was determined to see him brought to justice. Ireton enthusiastically accepted his appointment as one of the judges to try the King and, having found his sovereign guilty, added his own name and seal to the death warrant. Following the King's death,

Henry Ireton

Ireton served under Cromwell in Ireland where he became Lord Deputy, but in 1651 he died of swamp fever. His body was brought back to London and buried with great pomp and ceremony in the Henry VII Chapel of Westminster Abbey.

With the restoration of the Monarchy in 1660, even regicides already dead were not allowed to escape punishment and public humiliation. With gruesome ruthlessness, Ireton's body, along with those of Cromwell and Bradshaw, were exhumed and taken to Tyburn where they were hanged until sunset. Their bodies were then buried in a deep pit under the gallows, whilst their heads were put on public display outside Westminster Hall.

WILLIAM CAVENDISH OF WELBECK

Welbeck Abbey was acquired in 1597 by Charles Cavendish, a son of Bess of Hardwick. His eldest surviving son William Cavendish (b. 1592) lived there in supremely comfortable style during the reign of James I, and entertained on an unimaginably lavish scale that matched his ambition to hold high office. Cavendish received a number of titles during his long life. He was first created a Knight of the Bath, then Viscount Mansfield (following a royal visit to Welbeck in 1619), Earl of Newcastle in 1628, and Marquis in 1643. He was held in high esteem at the Court of Charles I, and for six years was Governor to the future Charles II, turning him into a very accomplished horseman.

William Cavendish, Duke of Newcastle

At the outbreak of the Civil War Cavendish, the Earl of Newcastle, was the officer commanding the King's armies in the north of England, with his headquarters in York. At first he revelled in his romantic role as a Royalist leader, enjoying the *'pomp and absolute authority of a general'*, but as the war progressed he grew tired of the burdens of responsibility and the sheer physical fatigue associated with soldiering.

By November 1642, Newcastle had amassed an eight thousand strong army and with it occupied York. Throughout 1643, with the Royalists well in command in the north of England, Newcastle threatened to advance on Nottinghamshire as part of the King's projected advance on London. With Nottingham Castle the only real obstacle in Newcastle's path, its governor, Colonel Hutchinson, prepared for the worst. Nottingham was an isolated Parliamentarian centre, surrounded by garrisoned Royalist manor houses including Newcastle's own at Welbeck. With Nottingham's people showing massive indifference, its crumbling castle looked an easy target.

On four occasions in 1643 Newcastle tried to move south and take Nottingham, but with good fortune almost beyond belief, the town remained untouched. The first of these attempts in January 1643 was thwarted when Sir Thomas Fairfax retook Leeds and Wakefield, causing Newcastle to return with his army to York.

In March, Newcastle threatened his second advance. The Parliamentarians hurriedly assembled a defensive force of 6,000 men from East Midland counties. Among them was Oliver Cromwell, whose imposing figure was frequently seen in Nottingham Market Place and the Castle Yard. By now the Royalists had reoccupied Wakefield and were again ready for an assault on Nottingham. Before this could happen, Fairfax had attacked Wakefield for a second time, taken 1,400 prisoners and sent Newcastle scurrying back to Yorkshire once more.

In June, Newcastle decisively defeated Fairfax at Adwalton Moor, near Bradford, a victory for which he was made a Marquis by his grateful King. With the north back in a firm Royalist grip, Newcastle threatened Nottingham a third time, issuing a summons to Colonel Hutchinson to surrender. *"If my lord would have that poor castle, he must wade to it in blood"* was the uncompromising reply from the governor's brother, George Hutchinson. But with trouble brewing in Hull, Newcastle retreated northwards yet again and Nottingham breathed a further sigh of relief.

Nottingham Castle, 1642

At the end of 1643, Newcastle was back at Welbeck and posing yet another major threat to the county town. Hutchinson was offered a bribe of £10,000 and a title by Newcastle, to surrender the castle but with the Governor and his men preparing to die behind the battlements, the hand of fate intervened yet again. The Scottish army, siding with the Roundheads, marched southwards forcing Newcastle's hasty return to defend York against this approaching menace from north of the border.

Prince Rupert

By April 1644, Royalist supremacy in the north had ended. Newcastle became besieged in York, surrounded by hostile Roundhead forces - a combination of the Scots and Sir Thomas Fairfax's army. Prince Rupert came to Newcastle's aid and, as he had done so successfully in Newark a month earlier, ended the siege. But with characteristic impetuosity, Rupert chased after the retreating enemy. Ignoring Newcastle's advice not to fight, the King's nephew committed his men to battle on Marston Moor.

The result was a massacre with 4,000 dead including the finest of Newcastle's 'Lambs' - so named because of their undyed woollen coats. Newcastle was utterly demoralised at seeing the army he had so carefully formed, wiped out at a stroke.

The war-weary Marquis was convinced that all was lost. Prince Rupert tried to reassure him otherwise but Newcastle, unable to face the certain ridicule that was to follow, turned tail and sailed for the continent.

He set up a riding school in Paris and was frequently visited by the exiled Charles II. In the 1620s he had built magnificent stables at Welbeck, and his knowledge of horsemanship is reflected in two books which he later wrote on the subject. In 1645 he married his second wife Margaret Lucas, a notable English writer of her day and sister of the Royalist soldier, Sir Charles Lucas. She published a famous biography of her husband in 1667.

After the Restoration, Cavendish played little role in public affairs and returned to Welbeck to recover his estates and rebuild his reputation. He was created Duke of Newcastle in 1665. Following his death eleven years later, he was buried in Westminster Abbey.

Welbeck during the Civil War was a Tudor mansion incorporating sections of the monastic cloisters of the old abbey buildings. In December 1642, the house was fortified and garrisoned for the King. It saw little action whilst the Royalists were in full control of the north, but with their emphatic defeat at Marston Moor in 1644 all this changed. Welbeck immediately fell to the Earl of Manchester's Roundheads who based 200 men there to keep a check on Newark. Raiding parties from Newark

Taking Welbeck

made a number of unsuccessful attacks on the house until July 1645. A Walloon from Belgium, Major Jammot, successfully hid himself and his troop of horses among the trees and bushes surrounding the house. Under cover of darkness they escaped the notice of scouts patrolling the estate. The scouts were about to re-enter the house as dawn broke, when Jammot's riders charged, leaping on to the partially raised drawbridge. With several guards thought to be in league with the Royalists, it was not too difficult for Jammot to retake the garrison. The 200 prisoners captured were taken to Newark. Their replacements, under Colonel John Frescheville, who became Governor of Welbeck, included Cavaliers from Pontefract and Scarborough Castles, both of which had just surrendered.

Welbeck remainded under Royalist occupation until disgarrisoned on 6th November 1645.

FRANCIS HACKER OF EAST BRIDGFORD

Colonel Francis Hacker was the eldest of a family of seven children. His father lived in East Bridgford (probably where Francis was born around 1618) but later built a house at Colston Bassett. Young Francis was the only member of his family to support the Parliamentarians, two of his other brothers being ardent Royalists. Thomas Hacker was killed in a skirmish at Colston Bassett, whilst Rowland Hacker became a captain in the King's army and for a while commanded a Royalist fort erected at Trent Bridge. He later lost an arm defending Newark.

At the young age of fourteen, Hacker married Isabel Brunts, a distant relative of Samuel Brunts, the benefactor of Brunts Charity in Mansfield. They had a son and four daughters.

Francis Hacker inherited Stathern Hall (destroyed at the end of the 17th Century) which stood at the east of the church on Mill Hill, overlooking the Vale of Belvoir. He was the Constable in the village and, apart from ensuring that the ale brewed in the village was up to assize standards, it was one of his duties to collect *'ship money'*, the tax which caused considerable discontent and which did much to discredit Charles I.

Colonel Francis Hacker

In 1643, Hacker was a militia commander in Leicestershire, the scene of most of his Civil War exploits. He was taken prisoner in November of that year, but released a month later in exchange for a Royalist colonel. He was imprisoned again in 1645 after the Cavaliers had captured Leicester. After a lengthy stay in the dungeons of Belvoir Castle, he was *'offered his pardon and the command of a regiment to change sides'* only to *'refuse it with scorne'*. In 1648 Hacker commanded the left wing of Colonel Rossiter's victorious Parliamentary forces at Willoughby.

When King Charles I was in custody during his trial, Hacker had the responsibility of looking after him, which he appears to have done with untypical civility. After the death sentence was pronounced, an order had to be signed for the execution itself. This warrant was directed to *'Colonel Francis Hacker, Colonel Huncks and Lieutenant Colonel Phayre and to every of them'*. It required them to ensure that the King was beheaded on January 30th, between ten in the morning and five in the afternoon. When it came to the actual signing, Colonel Huncks lost his nerve and refused. Even the cajolings of Cromwell, Ireton and Daniel Axtell, the Commander of the Whitehall guards, were to no avail. Francis Hacker needed no persuasion to sign, an act which later cost him his life.

To Collonell ffrancis Hacker Colonell Huncks and Lieutenant Colonell Phayre on & to every of them.

Execution Warrant

With all arrangements in place, the boy from East Bridgford accompanied the King at the head of the sombre procession as it made its way across St. James' Park to Whitehall. The King noticed that the block was very low and asked Hacker if a higher one could be provided, but nothing could be changed now. After a short speech delivered quietly to the group assembled on the scaffold, the King placed his head on the block while Hacker passed the axe to the executioner ....

Over the next eleven years Hacker remained a staunch supporter of Cromwell, commanding his militia to patrol Nottinghamshire, and searching out conspiracies against the Protectorate. In March 1655, with supporters of the secret 'Sealed Knot' active in the county, Hacker's men discovered a wagon, full of weapons, in a barn at Farnsfield. They demanded full explanations from the prisoners taken.

Hacker was a member for Leicestershire in Richard Cromwell's parliament but contributed little - *"all that hath known me have not known me to have been a man of oratory and God hath not given me a gift of utterance"*.

With Charles II's return from exile in 1660, two of the signatories of the execution warrant, Colonel Hacker and Daniel Axtell, were arrested and put on trial. Hacker made no attempt to deny the part he had played, his only defence being that *"I was a soldier and under command, and what I did was that by commission"*. The court called for the execution warrant to be produced. Hacker's wife duly obliged, thinking that it would prove that he was only acting under orders.

In the judges view, the warrant demonstrated that Hacker had acted neither ignorantly or unwittingly. Giving evidence against the two men to save himself was Colonel Huncks, who had declined to sign the warrant. Axtell and Hacker were doomed.

At nine, on the morning of 19th October 1660, the prisoners were taken to the gallows at Tyburn. With the speechmaking left to the more articulate Axtell, both men faced their execution with dignity and courage.

EDWARD WHALLEY OF SCREVETON

For centuries, generations of the Whalley family lived at Screveton. The church has a monument to Richard Whalley who had twenty-five children by his three wives, and who was admired by Henry VIII. A descendant of this noble knight was Edward Whalley, a wealthy woollen draper. He lived at Kirketon Hall which stood on the site of the present rectory until about 1823. Whalley's father had married an aunt of Oliver Cromwell and thus Edward and Cromwell were cousins.

Kirketon Hall, Screveton

Edward Whalley joined the Parliamentarians from the outset. He took part in many major battles throughout the Civil War, quickly rising among the ranks. He was a Major under Cromwell at Gainsborough in 1643 and a Lieutenant Colonel at Marston Moor in 1644. When Cromwell formed his New Model Army in 1645, Whalley was given command of one of its two sections, leading it with distinction at the Battle of Naseby that year. For his abilities he was appointed Colonel under Sir Thomas Fairfax. Parliament rewarded him several times. For capturing Banbury after an eleven week siege he received £100 to purchase two horses, and following the surrender of Worcester in 1646 was given the manor of Flawborough in Nottinghamshire, earlier confiscated from the Marquis of Newcastle.

In November 1647 Sir Thomas Fairfax sent Whalley to guard the King, who was by then imprisoned at Hampton Court. Whalley had received a warning note from Cromwell urging him to *''have a care of your guards''* who were rumoured to be planning an attempt on the King's life. It might readily be assumed that Whalley saw that the best way of protecting the King was by allowing him to escape! *'The back stairs and vault towards the water side'* presented the King with a route to freedom which he eagerly grasped. Whalley was left with a letter of thanks from the King signed *'Your friend, Charles R'* - and much explaining to do!

During the second Civil War, Whalley fought alongside Fairfax at Maidstone, and took part in the siege of Colchester.

On the 6th January 1649 Whalley was appointed as one of the 'judges' to try the King. Present throughout the trial, he was fourth to add his neat signature to the death warrant immediately below those of John Bradshaw, Thomas Grey and Oliver Cromwell.

A talented military leader, with an insatiable desire for action, Whalley fought for Cromwell at the Battle of Dunbar in 1650 and again at the Battle of Worcester a year later, which signalled the end of the Civil War, the end of the monarchy (albeit only temporarily) and the beginning of a political life for Screveton's most famous son.

These were turbulent times for Cromwell. In 1655, he attempted to provide stability for the country and more protection for himself by dividing the nation into eleven districts, each with a Major-General at its head. Edward Whalley was one of these, taking charge of Lincolnshire, Leicestershire, Derbyshire, Nottinghamshire and Warwickshire. His son-in-law, William Goffe, another signatory of the King's death warrant, was also a Major-General. Generally regarded as interfering busybodies, mainly concerned with closing ale houses and taxing Royalists to the point of persecution, the Major-Generals were hardly popular.

With Cromwell's death in 1658 followed by Richard Cromwell's complete ineffectiveness as leader, the time was ripe for the Restoration of the Monarchy. Edward Whalley and William Goffe deemed it prudent to disappear. In the certain knowledge of their fate as regicides if they remained, they left for Switzerland. By 1663, their whereabouts were discovered.

With a hefty price tag on their heads, the two men sailed to America and sought refuge amongst the Puritan descendants of the Pilgrim Fathers. The fugitives were well looked after at the friendly settlement of Cambridge, New England, but with the government of Charles II pledged to pursue the two men relentlessly, they were forced to go into hiding. At West Rock they built a hut with an old hatchet they had found. When danger threatened they transferred to a cave, where for four years, a woodman regularly supplied them with their daily bread and other necessities of life. When this became unsafe they hid in the cellar of the Governor of Newhaven Colony. They finally found respite from their persecutors when, after night-time marches through woods and forests, they reached Hadley. Here the local pastor concealed them in his cellar for eight miserable years.

In 1674 Goffe wrote to his wife in England. He described Whalley as still alive but extremely infirm. ''He is scarce capable of any rational discourse, his understanding, memory and speech doth so much fail him .... but he patiently bears all things'' It is thought that Whalley died in 1675.

THE BYRONS OF NEWSTEAD

After the dissolution of the monasteries by Henry VIII, the Priory at Newstead was bought by Sir John Byron of Colwick for £800. "Little Sir John with the great beard" as he was quaintly known, transformed the religious building into a dwelling house, which remained in the Byron family until the 19th century. Few families could have supported the King more zealously than the Byrons, with seven brothers and an uncle all holding officer ranks.

Looking on as the King raised his Standard was the most notable of the Byrons, the eldest brother John, later to become the 1st Lord Byron. Born around 1600, he sat in Parliament during the last years of James I reign and the first years of Charles I. He was High Sheriff of Nottinghamshire in 1634. Sir John fought in the first major Civil War clash at Edgehill, where his uncle Sir Nicholas Byron was wounded. Prince Rupert's initial cavalry charge sent the Parliamentarians scattering in all directions. Unfortunately, Sir John Byron's men went charging after them instead of remaining to guard the Royalist foot soldiers who were then attacked from behind by Sir William Balfour. Among those killed was the King's Standard Bearer, Sir Edmund Verney.

Sir Nicholas Byron

In December 1642, Sir John and his brother Thomas, commandeered Fawley Court near Henley on Thames, the home of Bulstrode Whitelock, an eminent lawyer. Despite Sir John's strict orders to his soldiers to the contrary, the house was looted, the deer in the park killed, horses stolen and all the food and drink consumed. Whitelock's children, instead of being harmed by such events, were taken under the personal protection of Sir Thomas who thought it *'barbarous to harm such pretty children'*. Perhaps the premature deaths of his own two young sons brought about such compassion.

Sir Thomas Byron

Sir Thomas was the first Byron to become a victim of the war, but not at the hands of his opponents. On December 7th 1643 whilst in Oxford, he was violently attacked in the street by Captain Hurst, an officer of his own regiment, after an altercation over pay. Hurst faced a firing squad within the week, but Sir Thomas survived in lingering agony until the following February. After his death he was buried in Christchurch Cathedral, Oxford.

On New Year's Eve 1642 Sir John, then quartered at Reading, was forced to repulse a mob from Cirencester, intent on killing him. He and his men showed no mercy to his attackers, killing twenty of them and dispelling the rest. During this incident, *'Sir John got a noble scar in the face'* - a feature clearly shown in his portrait by William Dobson, an Oxford artist who painted many of the leading Cavaliers of the day.

Sir John Byron

Sir John's one clear success of the Civil War was his attack at Roundway Down in July of 1643. Adopting a cavalry charge of which Prince Rupert would have been proud, Sir John put to flight Sir Arthur Hazelrigg's troops who fled *'over the downs in Bristol till they came to a precipice where ...... they gallop't down it as if it had been plain ground, and many of them brake both their own and their horses necks'*.

The barbarous streak in Sir John's nature manifested itself all too clearly during an incident in Cheshire. Villagers at Barthomly had sought refuge in the church, but after being smoked out by Byron's men, they were callously slaughtered. Writing to William Cavendish, Byron said *"I find it the best way to proceed with these kind of people for mercy is cruelty"*.

Sir John was to see little more success in the frays to come. Besieging Nantwich he managed to lose fifteen hundred prisoners and all his guns at the hands of Sir Thomas Fairfax. At Marston Moor he commanded Prince Rupert's right wing but following his own instincts led his men to meet Cromwell's charge and was routed in the process. Attempting to recapture Montgomery Castle he suffered heavy losses at the hands of Sir William Brereton. With admirable tenacity he did cling on to Chester in 1646 until good terms for its surrender had been agreed. He took charge of Caernarvon Castle until the King's surrender at Kelham led to all Royalist-held fortresses being given up. An effort to take North Wales for the King in 1648 ended in failure after which Sir John spent the remaining four years of his life on the continent in exile - a man who could expect no pardon from Parliament.

Apart from Sir John and Sir Thomas, five other Byron brothers fought in the Civil War:-

Sir Richard became Governor of Newark after leading a nearly-successful attempt to take Nottingham from the Roundheads.

Sir Robert commanded a regiment at Naseby and later served in Ireland.

Sir Philip was killed defending York when the city was stormed during the siege there in 1644. He was buried in York Minster.

Sir William did fight in the War but few details of his life are known. It is thought he drowned at sea.

Gilbert (d 1654), the only brother not knighted, was governor of Rhuddlan Castle in North Wales. He was imprisoned at Belvoir Castle after the Royalist defeat in the skirmish at Willoughby Field.

Newstead Looted

Newstead Abbey was garrisoned for the King in 1642 but abandoned soon afterwards, and evacuated without bloodshed. The house was plundered in 1644 by a group of Nottingham Roundheads sent to collect food and money from Mansfield. Their convoy of carts laden with valuables from the Abbey was taken by surprise when a party of Derbyshire Royalists, led by Colonel John Frescheville, ambushed them in a narrow lane near Bestwood Park. In the 'little scuffle' which followed, the Colonel was left with a cut hand and seven of his soldiers killed.

For a short while, Colonel Francis Peirrepont held Newstead as a Parliamentary garrison but it was relinquished when found to have little strategic value for them.

GILBERT MILLINGTON OF FELLEY

Gilbert Millington's signature on the Death Warrant of King Charles I found him a permanent niche in history which his political conduct would not otherwise seem to merit. Millington lived at Felley House, acquired by his father Anthony, along with the ancient ruined priory, in 1604.

In 1639, Viscount Chaworth, then High Sheriff of Nottinghamshire, was forced to relinquish his public duties because of failing health. He successfully appealed to Parliament to allow his neighbour, Gilbert Millington, *'a gentleman who would not allow his Majesty's service to suffer'*, to carry them out instead. Millington represented Nottingham in the Long Parliament, relishing the pleasures to be had from public service but contributing very little actively to it. He proved himself to be a weak and unreliable man, his indecision and lack of loyalty hidden beneath a facade of boisterous bluster. His social position rather than his abilities enabled him to hold the centre stage of local political activity.

Parliamentarians like Hutchinson stood for strongly held Puritan principles. Millington, on the other hand, could invariably be found lending support to Hutchinson's opponents whilst *'pretending all kindnesses and service to the Governor'*.

Predictably, such hypocrisy drew scathing criticism from Lucy Hutchinson, spurred on by Millington's public antagonism towards her husband. Her Puritan morals deeply offended, she related how *"Millington and White .... married a couple of alehouse wenches to their open shame .... and some reflection on Parliament itself .... when Millington, a man of 60 professes religion and having but lately buried a religious matronly gentlewoman, should goe to an alehouse to take a flirtish girl of 16"*.

Throughout the years of Cromwell's rule, Millington sat in Parliament, but later he was put on trial as a regicide. Many regicides stood up heroically to the charges levelled against them, but Millington timorously squealed before his judges, fawning and humbling himself to excite feelings of pity towards him. He played on his deafness and old age (he was by then 76 years old) to avoid pleading at all. When pressed he opted for 'not guilty' on the grounds that, unlike Hacker, he hadn't been *'upon the scaffold murthering the King'*. The jury found him guilty and the court pronounced the death sentence on him. For reasons unknown, this was commuted to life imprisonment. Millington's final years are shrouded in the mists of obscurity - perhaps fittingly for such an undistinguished politician who caused trouble and discord wherever his shadow fell.

WILLIAM STAUNTON OF STAUNTON

William Staunton, whose ancestral line reached back to the days of William the Conqueror, was born in 1608. He married Anne Waring who bore him thirteen children, of whom only six survived.

Home was the Tudor Hall at Staunton, with its three gables of which only the central one has survived the Georgian alterations of 1794. It stood alongside the church, surrounded by trees and parkland.

On that blustery August day in 1642, William Staunton looked on with pride as the King's Standard was raised. Having pledged his support for the Monarch, Staunton followed the King to Shrewsbury and it was not long before he was fighting in the first major battle of the Civil War at Edgehill. He clearly impressed and was

Colonel William Staunton

given a Colonel's commission to raise a regiment of twelve hundred foot soldiers and a troop of horse from the outlying villages of eastern Nottinghamshire. His popularity and influence there made this task easier, although he himself had to stand the cost! It is easy to picture Colonel Staunton as the typical Cavalier - his pointed beard and moustache, his long dark hair, his horse colourfully bedecked with all the equine trappings associated with the King's men.

Colonel Staunton's regiment was based at Newark and served under Lord Belasyse during the town's final siege. Colonel Staunton himself had quarters at the Old White Hart only a hundred yards from the Governor's House. In 1645 King Charles and Lord Digby left Newark to join Montrose in Scotland. Staunton and his regiment accompanied them. It was in Yorkshire that they learnt that Montrose's army had been crushed and he himself was on the run. Digby and Sir Marmaduke Langdale took fifteen hundred men to assist Montrose, however they marched straight into defeat, with Digby escaping to the Isle of Man in a fishing boat. Staunton avoided this by returning to Newark with the King.

With the Colonel away, Staunton Hall was vulnerable to attack. Defended only by Mrs. Staunton, with a group of twenty servants and others too unfit for the military, it held little resistance when the approach of the Roundheads was signalled by the man keeping watch in the church tower. The mattresses and bolsters hastily rammed against the doors and windows were little defence against the cannon shot directed at the old Hall. Mrs. Staunton and her faithful supporters defended as best they could, raining musket fire down from the upstairs windows onto the enemy

outside. Two small cannon balls ripped through the oak front door making holes which are still there. Driven by frustration, the Roundhead leader yelled orders for the Hall to be set ablaze. Confronted by this threat Anne Staunton surrendered. She and her children made their escape on horseback across the fields to Bennington. Travelling via the Great North Road they eventually reached London.

Staunton under attack

Meanwhile the empty Hall was stripped of its furniture, and valuables, and timber was taken from the park. The church too suffered damage at the hands of the irreverent Roundheads. The house rapidly deteriorated and would have presented a sorry spectacle when, after the King's surrender, Mrs. Staunton was allowed to return to *'remain dureing such time as the said house shall be in repairing (as alsoe for security the house for the end noe waste or spoil may be made there) without any molestation'*.

For *'having borne arms for the King'* William Staunton was fined one thousand five hundred and twenty pounds by Parliament, a sum which was eventually halved on account of the damage done to the Hall and the property and timber which was taken from it.

At the end of the Civil War, Colonel Staunton settled down to family life again, but not for long. Broken in health and spirit, he died in 1656 aged 48 and was buried in the church. Sadly, there is no memorial there for this gallant Cavalier although his wife, Anne, does have a marble tablet on the wall near the altar.

THE SAVILES OF RUFFORD

Rufford Abbey was acquired by the Talbot family in 1537, and passed into the Savile family some ninety years later. The Saviles were wealthy Yorkshire landowners and Rufford gave them a large part of Sherwood Forest where they could follow their favourite pursuit of deer hunting.

Sir William Savile

Sir William Savile (1612-1644) pledged his total support to the King from the outset. So determined was he to obstruct the Parliamentary cause, that he ordered his family home at Thornhill, near Wakefield, to be burnt down to prevent its use as a garrison for the King's enemies. Savile was active in the early years of the war, being Governor of York and Sheffield until his sudden death in 1644. Savile left behind a young family and his pregnant wife, Lady Anne Savile. It was most unusual for women to feature prominently in the masculine world of warfare, but Lady Anne proved a notable exception. During the siege of Sheffield she directed events against the Roundheads, who eventually broke down the castle walls and forced her to surrender.

"This gallant lady, famous for her warlike actions beyond her sex, had been besieged by the rebels in Sheffield Castle, which they battered on all sides by great guns, tho' she was big with child, and had so little regard for her sex, that in that condition they refused a midwife she had sent for, the liberty of going to her".

Favourable surrender terms having been agreed, Lady Anne and her supporters left Sheffield with full military honours. She gave birth to a son the next day and retired to Rufford and family life.

Lady Anne Savile

Lord Halifax

Lady Anne's eldest son, George Savile (1633-1695), later became the Marquis of Halifax and the most distinguished member of the family. He remained steadfastly loyal to the Crown and supported the secret "Sealed Knot" in their attempts to restore the exiled King Charles II to the throne in 1655. On 8th March that year, Rufford Abbey was a local rendezvous for the intended nationwide Royalist uprising. Three hundred Royalists gathered overnight at the New Inn near Rufford Abbey, ready to march to York. With rumours spreading that the plot had been betrayed, the conspirators hurriedly dumped their weapons in a nearby pond and dispersed without incident. George Savile was in London at this time and thus distanced himself from these events with which he had much sympathy.

By showing loyalty to the Monarch, and steering a middle course between political extremes, Lord Halifax acquired the nickname 'The Trimmer' and was to become one of the most important politicians during the reigns of Charles II and James II. After his death in 1695 he was buried in Westminster Abbey.

Rufford Abbey

THE PIERREPONTS OF HOLME PIERREPONT

Robert Pierrepont, First Earl of Kingston upon Hull, was the son of Sir Henry Pierrepont of Holme Pierrepont Hall and Frances Cavendish, daughter of the redoubtable Bess of Hardwick.

When the Monarch and Parliament were at loggerheads during the early years of Charles I's reign, the Earl sat firmly on the fence. He is reputed to have declared *"If I take up arms with Parliament against the King or with the King against Parliament, let a cannon ball divide me between them"*. A strong desire to retain his immense wealth was undoubtedly responsible for him deciding not to take risks by supporting either side! But it was virtually impossible for anyone, especially the aristocracy, to remain neutral after the King had raised his Standard. Kingston, like most of his local counterparts eventually sided with the King who began the war as clear favourite to win it.

Earl of Kingston

The Earl fought resolutely at the Battle of Gainsborough in 1643, doggedly defending a house which was eventually set alight. He was captured by Lord Willoughby of Parnham and taken by pinnace* bound, ironically, for Kingston upon Hull, the only town in Yorkshire held by the Parliamentarians.

Soldiers Firing at Pinnace

As the small vessel made its way along the Trent, Royalists from Newcastle's army appeared on the river bank and began to open fire on their Roundhead prey. The Earl appeared on deck to try and stop the shooting but became a sitting target for a cannon ball aimed in his direction. The noble lord was literally cut in two, thus fulfilling his prophetic words. He was buried beneath the chancel of Cuckney Church.

The Earl had three sons. The eldest, Lord Newark, unsuccessfully attempted to sieze the county's store of arms and ammunition for the King early in 1642, but was thwarted by John Hutchinson.

The two younger sons, William and Francis, supported Parliament - a ploy perhaps to ensure that some of the Pierreponts finished up on the winning side? Francis was a Colonel in the Roundhead army based at Nottingham Castle although he did command the Parliamentarian garrison established for a short time at Newstead Abbey. William later became one of the county's representatives in Cromwell's Parliament of 1654, and was highly regarded for his *'wisdom and soundness of judgement'*.

---

* A small boat with oars and sails.

SHELFORD

Shelford Manor stands about a mile from Shelford Village on the road to Gunthorpe Bridge. The site was once occupied by a small 12th century Augustinian priory. With the dissolution of the monasteries in the 16th Century, it passed into the Stanhope family, who later became the Earls of Chesterfield. The priory was replaced with an imposing manor house. In 1643 it was fortified with ramparts, palisades, moat and drawbridge, and garrisoned for the King by Philip Stanhope, son of the First Earl of Chesterfield. At first, Shelford Manor saw relatively little action, although the garrison based there did join with the Newark Royalists for attacks on Nottingham in 1643 and 1644.

By the autumn of 1645, the Royalist cause was all but lost. The Parliamentarians became determined to take the remaining Royalist strongholds, which in Nottinghamshire meant Newark. The nuisance value of Shelford to the Parliamentarians couldn't be underestimated, and in October 1645 Colonel Hutchinson offered Philip Stanhope favourable terms for its surrender. Stanhope's reply was in the form of a threat to *'lay Nottingham Castle flat as a pancake'*. On Saturday, 1st November 1645 Hutchinson, General Poyntz and Colonel Rossiter along with their horse and foot soldiers assembled in the village. Colonel Hutchinson

was to stay overnight in Shelford village but on his arrival he and his men were met by a party of snipers who had climbed into the church tower with a small cannon, drawing up the ladder and bell ropes as they went. The snipers refused to come down when Hutchinson threatened them, so he smoked them out by setting fire to straw at the foot of the church tower. The ploy worked and the dejected group were taken prisoner. They are said to have included a woman corporal and a boy who had once been in Hutchinson's own company. Hutchinson withdrew his death threat on the boy for changing sides, when the lad offered to disclose weaknesses in the defences at Shelford Manor.

Shelford Church Tower

The following day General Poyntz made preparations to take the Manor House, which was guarded by some two hundred of Colonel Stanhope's Cavaliers. On Monday 3rd November, Poyntz gave Stanhope half an hour to reply to his ultimatum to surrender. Stanhope remained steadfastly defiant, *''I keep this garrison for the King and in defence of it I will live and die''*. At four o'clock that afternoon Poyntz gave the order for battle to commence, and for half an hour fierce hand fighting took place in the grounds with Royalist musketeers firing down from the ramparts and the windows of the Manor. The Roundheads, assisted by a regiment of Dragoons from London under the command of Colonel Webb, gradually gained the upper hand. Poyntz, worried that Royalist reinforcements might arrive at any time from Newark, ordered that *'no quarter be given'* and the house was stormed. Forty men were killed on the staircase alone, with the fighting fierce and brutal. The activity was frenetic, and with the danger of Roundhead killing Roundhead, Poyntz commanded the slaughter to stop.

General Sydenham Poyntz

Over forty Royalists were taken prisoner and around one hundred and sixty were slain, including *'several gentlemen of the neighbourhood'*. The Roundhead claim to have lost only sixteen men would appear to be considerably understated given the ferocity of the fight.

Captain Philip Stanhope's end was singularly undignified. Shot and badly wounded during the fight he was, according to Lucy Hutchinson's account, stripped naked and *'flung upon a dunghill'*. Colonel Hutchinson's brother took the Shelford Governor to his own quarters, but despite the efforts of a surgeon Stanhope died the following day.

Shelford Ablaze

Several hours after the fighting ended, the night sky was aglow as flames engulfed the once magnificent seat of the Stanhope family. Whether accidentally or deliberately is not known. Lucy Hutchinson thought that *'the country people who had bene sorely infested by that garrison, to prevent the keeping of it by those who had taken it, purposely sett it on fire'*.

As Shelford burned, King Charles rode out of Newark heading via Belvoir for the comparative safety of Oxford.

The present day Shelford Manor dates from c.1676 and incorporates parts of the old ruins.

WIVERTON

With Shelford taken, Poyntz immediately headed for the neighbouring Royalist garrison at Wiverton Hall. The moated manor house, home of Lord John Chaworth, had been garrisoned for the King since January 1643.

Queen Henrietta Maria had slept overnight at the house in 1643. Prince Rupert, his brother Prince Maurice, Sir Richard Willys and 200 of their followers also stayed at Wiverton after the famous quarrel with the King at the Governor's House in Newark.

The Hall was defended by two v-shaped mounds called 'half-moon batteries' built on either side of the old approach road to the gatehouse, with its towers and Jacobean archway.

Initially, the governor, Sir Robert Therrill, was full of defiance towards Poyntz and his army. As the Roundheads were about to storm the house Therrill, with thoughts of Shelford's recent fate in his mind, *'yielded upon termes'*. The departing Royalists left behind them 150 firearms, 40

Wiverton Gatehouse

pikes, 3 barrels of powder, bullets and match, not to mention *'3 great vessels of beer'*! The strength of the garrison was such that Poyntz might well have felt relieved that a surrender without bloodshed had been achieved.

The Hall was immediately demolished to prevent any further use as a garrison but the gatehouse survived and was later incorporated into the present day Wiverton Hall, built in 1814.

SOUTHWELL

THE SARACEN'S HEAD

With the Parliamentary victory at Naseby in June 1645, Prince Rupert's surrender of Bristol three months later followed by Montrose's defeat in Scotland, the Royalist cause was crumbling fast. King Charles was in Oxford in March 1646, when he finally acknowledged the defeat that was staring him in the face. He decided to surrender to the Scots who, having subjected Newark to a bitter winter of siege, were continuing to hold it in a vice-like grip.

Saracen's Head, Southwell

King Charles, disguised as a clergyman, with his hair cut short and beard removed, left Oxford on the 26th April 1646. He travelled through the night from Stamford to Southwell, where at 7.00 a.m. on the 5th May 1646 he arrived at the King's Arms Inn, now called the Saracen's Head. The King rested in the downstairs room to the left of the archway. He had dinner with two Scottish commissioners and then gave himself up to them. That afternoon he was escorted along the road through Upton to 'Edinburgh', the Scottish headquarters established near Kelham Bridge. Here he remained as the prisoner of General David Leslie.

There is a certain irony in that it was at the Saracen's Head that King Charles I stayed in 1642 on his way to raise his Standard in Nottingham, which signalled the beginning of the Civil War.

General David Leslie

THE MINSTER

During the Civil War, the nave of the Minster was used not only to stable horses but also as a military store. A local Parliamentarian of the time was Edward Cludd (who later built a *'pretty brick house'* in Norwood Park, to the south of the present day Hall). Cludd is reputed to have encouraged the Scots to use the Archbishop's Palace as their residence in 1645. They showed scant respect for the building and it soon became vandalised, with lead being stripped from the roof and local residents removing stone and wood for their own use.

Following the King's surrender at Kelham, the Parliamentarians issued orders for the pulling down of places which might be fortified and used against them. These included the Archbishop's Palace and the Minster. The Palace was already in a ruinous state but the Minster itself was saved from certain destruction by the timely intervention of Edward Cludd, who used his influence with Oliver Cromwell to allow it to remain.

Old Archbishop's Palace, Southwell

WILLOUGHBY

On 3rd June 1648, Pontefract Castle in Yorkshire was captured by King Charles' supporters and this attracted many Nottinghamshire Royalists to gather there. However, within several weeks the garrison had become so large that shortages of food led to discontent amongst the men. Three hundred horsemen led by Sir Philip Monckton, and including Gilbert Byron of Newstead and Michael Stanhope of Shelford, went on the rampage, gathering support as they plundered their way southwards via Doncaster and Lincoln. On reaching Newark early in July their numbers had swelled to around eight hundred men.

By 3rd July, a Parliamentarian force of some six hundred horsemen, led by Colonel Edward Rossiter, was in hot pursuit. On reaching Owthorpe on 4th July, some of Monckson's men raided Colonel Hutchinson's house but with Rossiter only a few miles behind they took only food, a horse and a groom. The following day Rossiter's advance guard led by Captain Henry Champion caught up with the Royalists near Widmerpool where a running skirmish took place. The two main forces eventually clashed in combat at Willoughby, possibly in a field one hundred yards north-west of the Church. An alternative site may have been a field three quarters of a mile to the north-east of the Church.

Battle at Willoughby

The superior numbers of the professional Parliamentarian forces commanded from the centre by Colonel Rossiter and on the left flank by Colonel Francis Hacker, routed the inexperienced Royalists in the fierce battle which followed. The King's men eventually turned on their heels and fled in disarray. Many were later rounded up and taken prisoner (including Monckton and Byron) but Michael Stanhope along with one hundred Royalists and thirty Parliamentarians were killed. Both Rossiter and Hacker were wounded in the skirmish, the former insisting on remaining on his horse throughout so as not to discourage his own men.

According to tradition, inquisitive villagers scrambled into the church tower to gain a grandstand view of the battle which effectively marked the end of the second Civil War in Nottinghamshire. On the floor of the church, a small brass plate marks the final resting place of Michael Stanhope, who was *'slayne in Willoughby Field in the month of July 1648, in the 24th yeare of his age being a souldier for King Charles the First'*.

Colonel Edward Rossiter

THURGARTON

Following the dissolution of the monasteries, the Priory at Thurgarton came into the possession of the Cooper family. The church, stables and house were garrisoned for the King early in January 1643. However, the forty men there under Sir Roger Cooper saw little action for nearly two years, until the end of 1644 when they *'lined the hedges with musketeers'* and fired on Roundhead soldiers marching from Mansfield to Newark, killing their captain. In retaliation Colonel Thornhagh immediately took a party of Nottingham Roundheads to storm the church and stables at Thurgarton. The garrison quickly surrendered and the men taken back to Nottingham as prisoners.

NORWELL

On several occasions during the autumn of 1644, Newark Royalists had come under attack from Colonel Rossiter's men. Colonel Thornhagh too had led Roundhead raiding parties - the garrison at Thurgarton being a victim of their attentions. The Royalists, anxious to reinforce their hold on the area to the north of Newark, garrisoned Gervase Lee's moated house at Norwell in February 1645, and defended it with sixty men. Within days the Parliamentarians laid siege to the house and maintained their hold on it for three weeks. The siege ended when Colonel Rossiter required these forces to take on Sir Marmaduke Langdale's Cavaliers at Melton Mowbray. Gervase Lee stayed in Newark *'for the preservation of his health'*, during the siege of his house.

The house has long since gone but the moat survives to the south of the church.

COSTOCK

Bringing supplies into Nottingham was often a dangerous business with groups of Royalists scouring the countryside. The Parliamentarians were forced to travel in convoy and a favourite ploy to attack them was for musketeers to hide by the roadside and ambush the wagons and pack horses as they passed.

In September 1644, such a convoy snaked its way from Leicester to Nottingham. The Royalists, having stayed overlong in the local hostelries, failed to intercept it on its way in but were determined to attack it when it returned. They took up their positions in the hedgerows on the road between Rempstone and Costock, just north of where it crosses the Sheepwash Brook. As the convoy passed by, musket fire rained from the bushes. The surprised Parliamentarians quickly regained their poise and in the ensuing chaos, Lord Loughborough's Royalists were flushed from their roadside cover and chased across adjoining fields. A running skirmish developed

over Brickley Hill towards East Leake, resulting in eight Royalists killed and sixty taken prisoner. The visitors returned to Leicester that night '*with all their prisoners and prize, and were entertained with much joy and tryumph*'.

The parish register at East Leake Church, where the soldiers are buried under a slab near the porch, has the following entry:-

'*1644 ffoure souldiers buryed slaine in a skirmish in our lordship September ye 17th between partyes of the King's forces and the Parliament's whereof two were of his Majesties forces of Ashby de la Zouch garison and two of Leicester the Parliament's garison*'.

With soldiers from both sides patrolling Nottinghamshire, many minor skirmishes took place at various locations throughout the county. Often villagers would have to give 'free quarter' to troops, who stayed at their houses, ate their food and killed their animals. Accounts of the time record that pillaging and looting by drunken soldiers was commonplace and brought disruption to village life. Most country folk little cared which side won or lost as long as they could be left alone. By 1660, after years of heavy taxation and upset, they yearned for the peace that was to come with the Restoration of King Charles II.

Village Scene

A CHRONOLOGY OF THE ENGLISH CIVIL WAR

22nd August 1642	- King Charles raises his Royal Standard at Nottingham
23rd October 1642	- Battle of Edgehill
December 1642	- Sir John Henderson becomes Governor of Newark
January 1643	- Shelford, Thurgarton, Wiverton and Belvoir garrisoned for the King
27th-28th February 1643	- First Siege of Newark
21st June 1643	- Newark Royalists' attempt on Nottingham
16th June - 3rd July 1643	- Queen Henrietta Maria and her Royalist army stay at Newark
September 1643	- First Battle of Newbury
18th September 1643	- Royalists attack Nottingham
October 1643	- Sir Richard Byron becomes Governor of Newark
16th January 1644	- Newark Royalists attack Nottingham
29th February 1644	- Second Siege of Newark begins
21st March 1644	- Prince Rupert relieves Newark
2nd July 1644	- Battle of Marston Manor
2nd August 1644	- Welbeck surrenders to Parliamentarians
October 1644	- Second Battle of Newbury
December 1644	- Parliamentarians take Thurgarton Priory
January 1645	- Sir Richard Willys becomes Governor of Newark
February 1645	- Norwell House garrisoned for the King but besieged by Parliamentarians
March 1645	- Parliamentarians attack Staunton Hall
April 1645	- Royalists attack Nottingham
14th June 1645	- Battle of Naseby
16th July 1645	- Royalists retake Welbeck
October 1645	- King Charles at Newark; quarrel with Prince Rupert
3rd-5th November 1645	- Shelford and Wiverton taken by Parliamentarians (both houses destroyed)
4th November 1645	- Lord John Belasyse becomes Governor of Newark
6th November 1645	- Welbeck disgarrisoned and slighted
26th November 1645	- Third Siege of Newark begins
5th May 1646	- King Charles surrenders to the Scots at Kelham
6th May 1646	- Newark surrenders by order of the King

A CHRONOLOGY OF THE ENGLISH CIVIL WAR *(cont'd)*

24th June 1646	- Surrender of Oxford. **End of first Civil War**
3rd February 1647	- Charles handed over to English Parliament by the Scots
24th August 1647	- Charles taken to Hampton Court
11th November 1647	- Charles escapes to the Isle of Wight but imprisoned there at Carisbrooke Castle
5th July 1648	- Battle of Willoughby - effectively the end of the Civil War in Nottinghamshire
26th August 1648	- Surrender of Colchester
September 1648	- Battle of Preston
6th December 1648	- Colonel Pride's purge of the House of Commons
14th December 1648	- King Charles taken to Windsor
6th January 1649	- Act passed creating special court for King's trial
29th January 1649	- Death warrant issued
30th January 1649	- King beheaded outside Whitehall Palace
March 1649	- Surrender of Pontefract Castle and **end of second Civil War**
17th March 1649	- Monarchy abolished by Act of Parliament
September 1650 - September 1651	- **Third Civil War** fought for and by Charles II September 1650 - Battle of Dunbar September 1651 - Battle of Worcester

BOOKS FOR FURTHER READING

BENNETT, Martyn -
Travellers Guide to the Battlefields of the English Civil War
- Webb & Bower (1990)

MORRAH, Patrick -
Prince Rupert of the Rhine - Constable (1976)

ROYAL COMMISSION FOR HISTORICAL MONUMENTS (ENGLAND) -
Newark on Trent - The Civil War Siegeworks -
H.M.S.O. (1964)

SUTHERLAND, James (Editor) -
Lucy Hutchinson's Memoirs of the Life of Colonel Hutchinson -
Oxford University Press (1973)

TREASE, Geoffrey -
Portrait of a Cavalier (William Cavendish, 1st Duke of Newcastle) -
Macmillan (1979)

WEDGEWOOD, C.V. -
The King's War 1641-1647 - Collins (1958)

WEDGEWOOD, C.V. -
The Trial of Charles I - Collins (1964)

WOOD, A.C. -
Nottinghamshire in the Civil War - Oxford University Press (1937)

YOUNG, Peter -
The English Civil War Armies - Osprey (1973)

Also published by Nottinghamshire County Council:
Newark: Civil War and Siegeworks - Tim Warner
Discovering the Civil War in Nottinghamshire - Notts. Archives Office
The Civil War Colouring Book - Gillian Elias
The Civil War Puzzle Book - Gillian and David Elias